CAROL A. SANTAMAURA

Choosing *the* Right
Investment Advisor

iUniverse, Inc.
Bloomington

Choosing the Right Investment Advisor

The material in this publication is provided for informational purposes only. Given the evolving financial services landscape, regulatory requirements will change. This book is sold with the understanding that neither the publisher nor author is providing professional advice in this book—the content is intended to provide information and general guidelines only. It is always recommended that professional advice and support be obtained before acting on any information contained in this book.

iUniverse books may be ordered through booksellers or by contacting:

iUniverse
1663 Liberty Drive
Bloomington, IN 47403
www.iuniverse.com
1-800-Authors (1-800-288-4677)

Because of the dynamic nature of the Internet, any Web addresses or links contained in this book may have changed since publication and may no longer be valid. The views expressed in this work are solely those of the author and do not necessarily reflect the views of the publisher, and the publisher hereby disclaims any responsibility for them.

Any people depicted in stock imagery provided by Thinkstock are models, and such images are being used for illustrative purposes only.

Certain stock imagery © Thinkstock.

ISBN: 978-1-4620-5214-1 (sc)
ISBN: 978-1-4620-5216-5 (hc)
ISBN: 978-1-4620-5215-8 (e)

Printed in the United States of America

iUniverse rev. date: 10/21/2011

Author's Note

The principles outlined in *Choosing the Right Investment Advisor: An Essential Step on the Road to Financial Freedom* are directed primarily toward Canadian investors whenever referring to the banking system, regulators, and industry-related terminology.

However, the general content, as it relates to due diligence and good judgment, is universal.

To my clients: thank you for allowing me the privilege of earning your trust and confidence.

Investigate before you invest.
—attributed to Arthur Doyle Cobban (1895–1945)

All of the author's profits from the sale of this book will be donated to Princess Margaret Hospital, in honour of Jill Max.

About Princess Margaret Hospital

Toronto's Princess Margaret Hospital and its research arm, the Ontario Cancer Institute, have achieved an international reputation as global leaders in the fight against cancer. Clinical and research staff at PMH represent many of the world's leading experts, with specialties including surgical and radiation oncology. With each patient case, PMH combines state-of-the-art diagnosis and treatment with compassion and care. Our vision is to Conquer Cancer in Our Lifetime. For more information, please visit www.pmhf.ca.

CONTENTS

INTRODUCTION

Choosing the right investment advisor to help you with your finances is not a decision to be made lightly. Along with your health, family, and work, your financial well-being is one of the most important aspects of your life.

So, naturally, I am intrigued by the process used by individuals, families, and companies to select their advisors. Over the years, I have heard many investors discuss this topic. When I ask prospective clients and high–net worth investors how they selected their current advisors, I expect their answers to be based on the level of due diligence that a responsibility of this magnitude requires: quantitative criteria such as credentials, ethics, or returns. To my surprise, I am often answered with remarks like, "I met him at a party" or "he coaches my son's soccer team." One prospective client boasted that her advisor had been a professional athlete! On the other hand, I have met knowledgeable professionals over the years with sound investment management practices who have not succeeded in the industry. Investment management as a career can be highly lucrative. The more clients an advisor services and the more assets under his administration, the more money he makes. So how do you see past the charismatic salesman with a convincing pitch and determine whether he is a truly dedicated, ethical professional who will act in your best interest when managing your overall financial situation?

Managing your finances involves a lot of effort. You work hard to earn money, so you need to budget your expenses and set priorities for what you need and want in both the short-term and the longer-term. Shorter-term goals may include buying a house or funding your children's university expenses, while long-term goals may be funding your retirement or leaving a legacy to charities or to future generations. Even if you know where the money is going to come from, you have to find the best way to invest it in a risk-adjusted and tax-efficient manner.

It is for these reasons that taking care of your money can become a full-time job. While some investors attempt to manage their finances themselves, many high–net worth families realize that they do not have the time, the aptitude, or even the interest to do so. These investors often appreciate the value of professional advice and want to ensure that the individual whom they select is best qualified to handle this important aspect of their lives.

Finding the right person to help you manage your money and reach your financial goals can be a real challenge. Maybe you have sold a business, are a conscientious saver, or have benefitted from an inheritance. Regardless of how you have acquired your wealth, it is important that you manage it in the best way possible. Yet, on average, people spend more time in a year planning their holidays than they do on their finances. After all, it is your *financial security* we are talking about. One should not be so casual about such a critical decision.

The financial services industry has witnessed explosive growth over the last several years. Much of the difficulty in selecting an advisor lies in the increasingly complex and confusing nature of the industry. These days, it seems that everyone is a financial consultant of some sort, as the term is now broadly defined (e.g., investment advisor, investment executive, financial planner). There is also a substantial overlap in the products and services that can be provided by companies and individual advisors. Yet another challenge facing the average investor is that he may not fully understand what he needs or what advisors can provide.

To help you navigate your way through the complexities of the investment industry, this book as been divided into three parts. Part one will help you to understand what kind of investor you are and what kind of advice you need. Awareness of certain characteristics in your own behaviour as they relate to investing will help you with your decision to work with an advisor. It will also help to identify what kind of products and services you may need. For example, as a conservative investor, you many want a portfolio that is made up primarily of fixed-term investments with little volatility. Maybe you are a risk-taker who is willing to take on greater volatility through a portfolio of growth stocks. Or, perhaps, you are somewhere in between.

Part two provides you with some practical guidelines and useful tips to finding, evaluating, and working successfully with an advisor.

Part three examines the Canadian investment industry as we know it today, from companies and the services they provide, to the individual advisor, their qualifications, and the products they are licensed to sell.

Whether you are looking for an advisor or evaluating your present situation, this book provides you with a perspective on how to make an informed decision when choosing and working with the advisor who is right for you.

— CHAPTER 1 —
What Kind of Advice Do You Need?

Here are just a few of the investment-related services an advisor can provide for you, in addition to the trading of securities. The advisor can help you to

- establish your goals;
- build a plan;
- choose suitable investments;
- manage your portfolio;
- track your progress; and
- adjust your plan, when needed.

Historically, brokerage firms traded stocks, insurance companies sold insurance, and retirement plans were only available through financial-planning firms. Today, firms have evolved and many advisors are now in position to provide a broad range of advice and services. Here are some of the additional services that an advisor may be able to provide, either directly or through qualified members of his support team:

- discretionary investment management
- tax support (offered by a qualified consultant)
- financial planning
- will and estate consultation (offered by a qualified consultant)
- insurance solutions (if advisor is qualified)
- trust services

Everyone requires a certain amount of advice. While some try to manage their investments on their own, it is not always a priority, and finding the time can be a challenge. Busy people and those who have neither the aptitude nor the interest need advisors who can devote their time and full attention to the management of the clients' investments.

Perhaps you are a fully knowledgeable and sophisticated investor who only needs trade execution at the cheapest price. Maybe you are interested in the stock market and require access to research and someone with whom you can discuss your ideas. Many investors do not have the interest, time, or aptitude and want a qualified advisor who will make the decisions for them. Yet, they still want to be kept abreast of changes and would like to understand the decision-making process and be kept informed of changes to their accounts.

The depth of advice and kinds of products you will need will also be determined by where you are in your investing life. Generally, this can be broken down into three stages:

1. A wealth builder or accumulator
2. A wealth manager
3. A wealth harvester

Wealth Builder

The wealth builder is typically a younger individual, perhaps one who is just starting to raise a family and who is beginning to save for his future. At this point, the advice he needs may be centred around a financial plan, which will map his course of action to reach his financial goals. Some of the goals addressed in a financial plan are

- buying a home;
- funding his children's education needs;
- saving for a major expenditure, like a vacation property;
- buying insurance to protect his family;
- saving for retirement; and
- managing investments.

The services of a bank, financial planner, or mutual fund company should be able to meet the needs of most investors at this stage. The calibre of investment advice may be of lesser importance. The main goal here is to get organized and start saving.

Wealth Manager

The wealth manager is typically an investor who is in his last decade of working and is approaching retirement. He has paid off his mortgage and other debts and has substantial savings. At this stage, he may need the following services:

- retirement planning, to ensure he has accumulated enough wealth to cover expenses in retirement
- business succession planning, if he's a business owner
- tax planning
- investment management

As your assets grow and your needs become more complex, you may require a more sophisticated and custom-tailored approach to your overall wealth-management strategy. At this stage, the calibre of investment management becomes critical in ensuring long-term success. Under these circumstances, you may be better served by an advisor who works for a full-service brokerage firm or an investment counsellor.

Wealth Harvester

The wealth harvester is the retiree whose goals are to live comfortably and perhaps to leave a legacy to future generations. He may need some of the following services:

- income generation
- long-term care needs
- will and estate planning
- growth of capital for beneficiaries

HANDS-ON/HANDS-OFF

Once you have decided what kind of advice you need, you then need to consider how actively involved you wish to be in the day-to-day decision-making process in your account.

There are two types of investment relationships: those established on an advisory basis and those that work on a discretionary basis. In the former relationship, you must give your verbal confirmation before any trade can be executed. In a discretionary arrangement, a framework within which the advisor is to make decisions is set out beforehand. You are then removed from management of the account and the stresses that accompany daily involvement.

Portfolio or discretionary management is ideal for investors who

- desire customized and personalized service;
- want freedom from making daily investment decisions;
- seek a disciplined approach to professional investment management;
- wish to benefit from an arrangement whereby the advisor can implement changes immediately, without having to wait for client approval; or
- wish to benefit from bulk trades, meaning that a single order comprised of all of the advisor's clients' holdings can be entered, as opposed to one order per clients. The former approach results in better prices.

Regardless of your stage in life or of the products and services you may require, I do recommend you seek the advice of the qualified investment professional who is best suited to meet your needs.

— CHAPTER 2 —

Psychology 101:
What Kind of Investor Are You?

Awareness of your own personality type can help you to identify advisors with whom you are compatible, and research conducted on personality types has been adapted to understand different types of investors.

The method used by many management training programmes and employers is the Merrill-Reid method,[1] which categorizes personality types into four distinct categories:

1. Analytical people
2. Drivers
3. Amiable people
4. Expressive people

---

1   David W. Merrill and Roger H. Rcid, *Personal Styles and Effective Performance*, CRC Pre, 1981.

Analytical People

Analytical people are known for being systematic, well organized, and deliberate. These individuals appreciate facts and information presented in a logical manner. They enjoy organization and the completion of detailed tasks. At times, others may see them as being too cautious and overly structured.

Analytical people
- are highly detail oriented;
- can have a difficult time making decisions without all the facts;
- tend to be highly critical and/or pessimistic in nature; and
- are very perceptive.[2]

The analytical person is frustrated by the stock market because it is not an exact science. He feels that, because there are so many numbers, there must be a formula for calculating market outcome. Before making a decision, he requires the latest research report on the company of interest. He arrives at his annual review with a briefcase full of detailed graphs and charts.

Drivers

Drivers thrive on the thrill of the challenge and the internal motivation to succeed. They are practical people who focus on getting results. They are often decisive, direct, and pragmatic. Drivers are high achievers who are not averse to risk. These individuals are extroverted, strong-willed, forceful, and decisive.

---

2   Adam Hayes. "If You Only Understood Your Customer's Personality Styles." http://www.ahfx.net/weblog/37.

They are task, rather than relationship-oriented and want immediate results.[3]

A driver
- is objective-focused;
- knows what he wants and how to get there;
- communicates quickly, getting to the point; and
- is hardworking, has high energy, and does not shy away from conflict.

As an investor, the driver is quick to make a decision based on the information that he is provided. He is comfortable with taking calculated risks in his portfolio. He does not call his advisor often, but when he does, he wants answers to his questions immediately.

Amiable People

Amiable people are dependable, loyal, and easygoing. They like things that are nonthreatening and friendly. They hate dealing with impersonal details and cold, hard facts. Amiable people are usually quick to reach a decision. They are team players, cooperative, and easy to get along with. They are trusting, sensitive, and good listeners. That being said, they will often not speak up for themselves; they are too compliant and nice.[4]

Amiable people
- are kindhearted people who avoid conflict;

---

3   Ibid.
4   Adam Hayes. "If You Only Understood Your Customer's Personality Styles." http://www.ahfx.net/weblog/ 37, last accessed July 8, 2011.

- can blend into any situation well;
- are highly sensitive; and
- can be quiet and soft-spoken.

The qualities of an amiable person can make him the dream client for many investment advisors. Trusting by nature and quick to make decisions, the amiable client will often defer to the expertise of his advisor and will generally agree with the advisor's recommendations.

Expressive People

Expressive people are very outgoing and enthusiastic and have a high energy level. They are great idea generators, but they usually do not have the ability to see the idea through to completion. They are relationship rather than task oriented and may be overly dramatic and impulsive.

Expressive people
- are warm and enthusiastic;
- are good motivators and communicators;
- can tend to exaggerate or leave out facts and details; and
- would sometimes rather talk about things than do them.

Expressive clients are very personable and love to chat about their lives, their families, and noninvestment-related issues. One of the challenges with expressive people, as investors, is that they are often slow about making decisions. When an expressive investor is faced with a recommendation to change an investment in his account, his response is often, "Let me think about it and call you back." Usually, he does not follow up and, if he does, it is may be too late to benefit from the original suggestion. This indecision can, in turn, affect the overall returns in his portfolio.

Understanding your own psychology can put you in a better situation to evaluate the kind of advisor with whom you will be able to work. Ultimately, successful relationships, whether personal or business, are often based on a sense of affinity. Simply put, we tend to deal with people we like. The purpose of this chapter is to help you to identify your own psychology, which, in turn, should help you to select an advisor with whom you will find it easy to communicate—a crucial element in a successful partnership.

— CHAPTER 3 —
Understanding Risk

One of the most crucial—yet also the most complex—issues to define, as it relates to investing, is your tolerance for risk. Risk is a subjective term that means different things to different people. To some, risk is viewed as the possibility of losing all of their money. To others, risk may be the decline in purchasing power of their money if it does not keep pace with inflation. I have seen clients in their eighties who would define themselves as conservative despite the fact that their portfolios are made up of 100 percent equities. They have good, quality stocks and are unaffected by market volatility. This is because they have experienced many market cycles. I have also seen clients in their late forties who consider themselves conservative and have all of their money invested in fixed-term securities like guaranteed investment certificates (GICs) because they do not want to see the value of their capital fluctuate. Are you comfortable with periodic declines in the value of your account (say, one or two years of decline) if you can reasonably expect better returns over the longer term?

Risk Taker versus Risk Avoider

Fundamentally, there are two types of personalities regarding risk. Knowing which one you have is an important step in managing your investment portfolio properly.

Risk Taker

This is the type of person who lives for the thrill and loves to take a chance. He thrives on the element of danger and risk involved in his activities. He is at the greatest risk of losing money because of a poor investment. Risk takers are speculators who might invest in high-risk securities, such as junior mining companies or speculative options trading.[5]

Risk Avoider

This type of person is the conservative investor who never takes risks. Though he is likely to live a safe life, he is often unable to ever experience true wealth or any other rewards that are associated with taking risks. In order to get desired returns, it may be necessary to embrace some calculated risk in one's portfolio.[6]

Factors Influencing Risk in Your Portfolio

Risk is not only a function of personality type. Other factors contribute to how much risk an investor *can tolerate* and how much risk he *needs* to assume in his portfolio in order to reach his desired goal or outcome.

---

5   The Money Instuctor.com. "Understanding Risk." Accessed December 2010, http://www.moneyinstructor.com/art/risktypes.asp.
6   Ibid.

An investor's risk tolerance is influenced by his level of investment knowledge and experience. A sophisticated investor may be comfortable assuming a greater degree of risk because he fully understands the risk/reward paradigm. Someone who is new to investing may feel uncomfortable with market cycles and the associated volatility that the portfolio may experience.

How much risk an investor needs in his portfolio will be determined by his needs and objectives. For example, an older person with a high net worth may need little risk in his portfolio because he does not need to grow his capital. Someone with an objective of aggressive growth, on the other hand, may need to take on a greater amount of risk because he needs a potential return that cannot be met by low-risk, low-yielding investments, even though a higher degree of risk may also result in significant loss.

Given that risk can mean different things to different investors, it would be prudent for you to have a clear understanding of how your advisor defines risk and how that definition is applied to the ongoing management of your portfolio. Some advisors will define risk as an interim volatility of your investments or as a potential loss of capital. In the former definition, a security may fluctuate in value in the interim, but it is expected to increase in the long term. Loss of capital implies that the investment is highly speculative and could become worthless.

No matter what the definition, it is critical that your understanding of risk is aligned with your advisor in order to achieve the right balance between your risk tolerance and your desired investment outcome. A good advisor will always strive to make recommendations that are aligned to these fundamental guiding principles. In every successful client-advisor relationship, investors must trust that their advisor is making investment recommendations with the best intentions based on the information available at the time. That said, there could be times when a suitable investment could experience periods of underperformance.

— CHAPTER 4 —
Psychological Pitfalls to Investing

I discovered this article while conducting research and thought I should include it in my book.

As discussed in the previous chapter, psychology plays an enormous role in how we make investment decisions. Unfortunately, many of our natural psychological reactions—like denial, panic, or greed—can impede our long-term success.

Ask yourself the following questions: Do you get anxious when the stock market is volatile? Do you feel optimistic that everything will turn out fine? Both reactions, which are natural parts of your psychological makeup, can actually impede your progress in reaching your investment goals. Amateur investors often fail because they allow psychology to influence their decisions.

The following are some common psychological pitfalls of investing.

Optimism

People have a natural tendency to overestimate the likelihood of positive results on everything from the weather to investing. This largely explains why people are so often disappointed by their investment performance—they simply felt they would do better.

If you base your financial goals on unrealistically positive expectations, you will almost certainly fall short of these goals. This can affect your retirement date, amount of retirement income, or the value of your estate.

Overconfidence

Another powerful psychological bias is overconfidence. Just as people tend to be overly optimistic about the probability of positive results, they also tend to be overconfident about their own talents. Some investors think that they (or their advisor) can "outsmart the market" and even control largely unpredictable events such as stock market volatility.

This leads to one of the most common pitfalls of investing: market timing. Confident in their abilities, many investors try to time the market so that they always buy low and sell high, despite the fact that not even the most accomplished professional investors can do this consistently.

Hindsight

Hindsight is the tendency to believe, after something has happened, that you knew all along that it would even though you did not. This tendency can lead you to believe that events are far more predictable than they really are and raise unrealistic expectations about how well your investments will perform and about your advisor's ability to foretell the future, among other things. If you find yourself confidently declaring that you "knew it all along" ask yourself whether you really did.

Obsession

Do you follow the minute-by-minute performance of your investments on TV or the Internet? Do you focus on short-term changes in the market value of your investments? Do you fixate on the negative performance of a single investment, even when your overall portfolio is doing well? These can all be signs of obsessive behaviour commonly displayed by investors.

Denial

When stock markets go down, investors sometimes panic and sell what is still fundamentally a good investment. The flipside of this is denial—when investors continue to hold an investment that has gone bad, thinking it will eventually come back. It can be hard, but when an investment has fundamentally deteriorated, it may be time to sell. The right investment advisor will help you to implement an investment discipline with specific, rational criteria for buying and selling, which will help you to overcome this tendency.

GREED

The desire to get rich quick compels many investors to take bigger risks than they should, such as investing too much in a single investment. Greed can also manifest itself in a reluctance to sell a particular investment with a substantial gain for fear it could go even higher. This does not mean you should never take a risk; risk is a normal part of investing. The key is to take well-calculated risks within a properly diversified investment portfolio that has been designed with your personal risk tolerance in mind. That way, when the occasional risk does not pay off, the impact is mitigated by the other investments in your portfolio.

THE HERD INSTINCT

When we see other people doing something, we have a natural tendency to think that it must be a good thing, and so we do the same. This herd instinct is often behind sharp ups and downs in the financial markets. When other people are buying, propelling the market upward, we buy too, sending the market even higher. Similarly, when other people sell in a panic, sending the market downward, we might also sell, fuelling the decline. Unfortunately, this often results in buying at the height of the market euphoria or selling close to the depths of the panic. Instead of following the herd, follow a disciplined investment strategy based on logic and reason.[7]

Successful investing can be less about how the markets are doing

---

7   RBC Dominion Securities, "Seven Psychological Pitfalls to Investing and How to Avoid Them." Toronto, November 20, 2010.

than about how you react to them. The right advisor can help you to overcome your psychological barriers and take a well-balanced and objective approach to your investment strategy.

— CHAPTER 5 —
Interviewing Candidates

An easy way to begin your search for a new advisor is to ask for referrals from people you know. Studies have found that most people are more than willing to give referrals when asked. Start with family members, colleagues, and friends. You can also ask other advisors, like your accountant or lawyer, or professionals you may respect and deal with through business, boards, or charities.

No matter whom you ask, make sure to find out why they are recommending an advisor to you. Answers like "He seems like a nice guy" or "I played golf with her last week" are not strong enough endorsements of a person's skill or ability. Just because Uncle Harry has dealt with the same individual for twenty-five years does not mean that person is the right advisor for you. Everyone's personal goals and tolerance for risk are unique, as are expectations and ideas about what constitutes a good advisor. An accountant recommending an advisor whom some of his clients use, whose statements he has seen, and who has shown an ability to protect clients' principal in a market downturn—now that is a strong referral!

Today, many advisors have websites so you can get an idea of who they are and what kind of business they manage. If you are meeting with a registered advisor, you can research him on your local securities commission's website. There you will see their designations and, more importantly, whether they have been subject to any disciplinary actions. This will help you to reduce the risk of making a poor choice.

I always recommend you meet with each candidate personally. In the past, when advisors were predominantly order takers, this may not have been necessary. But today, you are giving the advisor a great deal of responsibility, so it is imperative you have at least one face-to-face meeting.

In addition to establishing a good fit with the individual advisor, you need to ensure that he works for a reputable firm. There are a number of basic questions you should ask about each advisor's employer. Make sure to familiarize yourself with the different financial service providers available in Canada (see chapter 10).

Important Questions about the Firm

- What kind of company is it? For example, is it a full-service brokerage firm?
- Why did the advisor chose to work for her firm?
- Who regulates the firm?
- What kind of services does the firm provide— investment management only or financial, estate, and

tax planning? Are you entitled to benefit from those services?

- Is the advisor limited to certain investments only (i.e., guaranteed investment certificates and mutual funds)? Are there investment products and services she cannot provide?
- What is the depth and quality of research support?

About the Advisor

Here are some helpful topics to address with each candidate when you meet with him.

Credentials (see chapter 11)

Ensure that the IA is properly qualified to provide the services you require. Many financial planners provide investment advice, but not all investment advisors are financial planners. Some financial planners assess every aspect of your financial life—including saving, investments, insurance, taxes, retirement, and estate planning—and help you develop a detailed strategy or financial plan for meeting all of your financial goals.

Others call themselves financial planners, but they may only be able to recommend that you invest in a narrow range of products.

Investment advisors and financial planners may come from many different educational and professional backgrounds. Before you hire a financial professional, be sure to ask about his background. If he has credentials, ask him what they mean and how they were earned.[8]

Experience

It is important for the prospective advisor to quantify how many years he has been managing money. If someone says he has twenty-five years in the financial services industry, make sure those twenty-five years were spent managing money and not as a commercial lender at the bank. Other noninvestment financial services experience is often irrelevant.

If possible, it is a good idea to find an advisor who has experienced both the ups and the downs of the market and who has lived through at least two full market cycles. This would typically be eight years at a minimum. Newer advisors tend to have all the theoretical knowledge but little real-life experience in the markets.

How Does the Advisor Get Paid? (see chapter 5)

Does the advisor get paid with a commission per transaction or with a fee based on the value of assets under management?

Client Base

Who is the advisor's typical client?

What is the demographic profile of his client base: retirees or younger people?

Does he focus on specific industry groups, like doctors for example?

---

8   Canadian Securities Administrators. "Working with a Financial Advisor." http://www.securities.adminstrators.ca/uploadedfiles/general/pdfs/choosing_advisors_brochure.pdf.

It can be reassuring to know that your advisor has other clients who have profiles and requirements similar to yours.

How Many Clients Does the Advisor Have?

Established advisors typically employ teams for greater efficiency and to ensure that all clients' needs are handled on a timely basis. Larger teams may be able to handle several hundred clients. Too few clients may be a potential red flag, so you will need to question your advisor further if he has a small client base. Likewise, an advisor who has too many clients may have little contact with you or provide insufficient personal attention.

Minimum Account Size

Some firms and advisors require a minimum account size for new clients. Make sure to find out if you qualify.

What Kind of Reporting Can You Expect?

Find out how often you can expect to receive a statement of your account.

Will the statements show your rate of return?

You are entitled to know exactly what your return has been, net of fees. On a yearly basis, you should be provided with a statement showing performance. You should also receive a comprehensive year-end tax package with a summary of all transactions for tax purposes.

How Often Should You Hear from Your Advisor?

How much contact can you expect? This question can be difficult to answer. The size and complexity of your account will have some impact on how much service and individual attention you will receive from your advisor. You should agree on a service plan with your advisor once you have made the decision to work with him. It is important for you to have a realistic expectation in this regard. As most service offerings are long term in nature, day-to-day contact may not always be required. Therefore, unless you are an active trader, it may be unrealistic to expect to receive frequent contact with research or recommendations.[9] The temptation to micromanage your account can be detrimental to the long-term success of your investment plan.

It is reasonable to expect some kind of quarterly contact. You should be contacted personally for any significant investment changes or major events in the market. I recommend a minimum of at least one annual comprehensive review per year. This can be conducted either face-to-face or by telephone.

How Much Activity Should I Expect?

This question is also difficult to answer. Even if you are paying a fee, it will not necessarily equate to frequent trading activity. There can be several months in which no changes are necessary to your account followed by times when many trades are executed. This is generally not a concern if you are paying a fee. Fee-based accounts, whether advisory or discretionary in nature, offer a number of services in addition to investment management and trade execution. However, you should watch for excessive trades in an account in which you are charged a commission per trade. Conversely, if you see no trades in your fee-based account, it is possible that your advisor is not paying close attention to your investments.

---

9   Canadian Securities Institute Global Education. "Choosing the Right Investment Advisor: Things You Should Know." https://www.csi.ca /student/en_ca/home.xhtml, accessed July 8, 2011.

Advisor's Investment Discipline or Strategy
- What is her fundamental approach to investing?
- What investment products does she use?
- What is her investment discipline?
- Does it make sense to you?
- Does the advisor use a time-tested discipline or just rely on gut instinct?

Will Your Capital Be Pooled or Segregated?

Even at the highest levels of discretionary management, it is important to distinguish between pooled funds and segregated funds. In the former, money is grouped together and managed as one pool of capital, as with mutual funds. Rather than owning a portfolio of individual securities, investors own units in the pool. Segregated management means direct investment in various kinds of securities, like stocks and bonds. This allows your advisor to custom-tailor your investments to suit your objectives. As your assets grow, so does your entitlement to a personalized portfolio. Customization is the ultimate level of investment management.

Rate of Return

Chapter 7 explains how to evaluate return. Make sure to ask how returns are reported and how performance is measured. While important, rate of return is only one of the many filters that should be used in evaluating an investment advisor. Several sections of this book have pointed out that performance cannot be guaranteed. However, long-term, historical data may indicate the advisor's experience in dealing with broad market conditions. As such, past performance should not be overlooked.

Questions for You

After you have personally met and interviewed all of the candidates, ask yourself three important questions about each of them.

Is the Advisor a Good Listener?

Naturally, you want to ensure that your advisor has the necessary credentials and experience. Yet, the ability to listen is one of the most important qualities in a good investment advisor. Every client is different and has different objectives, time horizons, and tolerances for risk. Your advisor should listen in order to be able to design and implement a portfolio strategy that is custom-tailored to your individual needs. This is how you will be able to build trust and confidence in your advisor over time. You do not want someone who takes a cookie-cutter or one-size-fits-all approach to investing. He should ask probing questions that help you tell the complete story.

Did the Advisor Talk at Your Level?

A good financial advisor is also a good teacher. After gauging your current level of financial knowledge, your advisor should be able to explain things in a language you can understand. Although some aspects of investing may appear complex, you should be able to understand the basic concepts as they apply to you.[10]

Is There a Good Fit?

After carrying out all of the required due diligence, do you feel confident that you can work with the individual over the long haul?

---

10   http://www.osc.gov.on.ca/documents/en/Investors/res_working-with
      -adviser_en.pdf, accessed July 8, 2011.

It is often said that individuals decide whether or not to work with someone within minutes of meeting him or her. Choosing the appropriate IA to manage your money requires careful thought and consideration. The purpose of this chapter is to provide you with some practical tools necessary to help you make an informed decision.

— Chapter 6 —
To Fee or Not to Fee: Understanding Costs

A dvisors are compensated in many ways. Typically, an advisor's commission is one of the following:

- an annual salary
- commission per transaction
- a flat fee based on an hourly rate
- an annual fee that is a percentage of the dollar value of investments under management
- some combination of the above[11]

The two most common forms of compensation available today are (1) commission per transaction and (2) annual fee.

---

11   http://www.osc.gov.on.ca/documents/en/Investors/res_working-with -adviser_en.pdf, accessed July 8, 2011.

COMMISSION PER TRANSACTION

In a commission-per-transaction arrangement, the advisor receives compensation on each trade. This includes commissions on trades executed on the stock exchange. It may also include commission on certain mutual fund purchases.

Some of the advantages of a commission-based arrangement are as follows:

- Commissions are paid only on transactions that are executed.
- No fees are charged on "legacy" (i.e., inherited) positions and positions that may never be sold.
- All transactions must be verbally approved by you, the account holder, prior to execution.

Commission-based arrangements are best suited for the investor who wishes to be intimately involved in the decision-making process in his account.

FEE-BASED ARRANGEMENT

Under a fee-based arrangement, an annual management fee, which is a percentage of the total dollar value of assets under management, is charged.

Some of the advantages of fee-based arrangements are as follows:

- They can be discretionary or non-discretionary.
- There is transparency of fees (i.e., the client knows exactly how much he is paying).
- The client doesn't have to pay commissions for multiple transactions.
- They eliminate any perceived or actual conflict of interest inherent in a fee-for-transaction arrangement.
- Some clients will not make changes to their portfolios, because they do not want to pay a commission, even if a recommendation is a sound one. In a fee-based account, this obstacle is overcome because there is no transaction cost per trade.
- Fees are tax deductible in some cases.
- Better rates are available on some fixed-income securities.
- The advisor's compensation is not affected by the number of trades in an account.
- There are no custodial fees.

If you do choose to go this route, make sure that the fee you are being charged includes all costs. Some advisors charge an annual management fee, in addition to trade-execution fees and safekeeping fees for your securities.

OTHER FEES

Here are some other fees relating to the products that may be recommended to you and to their ongoing management that you should be aware of:

Fixed Income

Investments like bonds do not charge a commission. The fee is imbedded in the price paid and can be incorporated into the yield.

Initial Public Offerings (IPO)

New issues, or initial public offerings, charge no commission, but the advisor shares in the compensation fees paid by the issuer, often up to 5 percent.

Principal Protected Notes

Principal protect notes (PPNs) like index-linked notes have become very popular over the last few years. These notes have no visible cost but do charge an ongoing management fee.

Mutual Funds

There are two different costs or fees associated with mutual funds that you should be aware of. The first charge relates to the purchase of the fund. The other relates to the ongoing management of the fund. I will examine both in detail.

There are three different ways to purchase mutual funds:

1. Back-end, or deferred sales charge (DSC)
2. Front-end, or low-load
3. No-load, or zero-load

1. Back-End, or Deferred Sales Charge (DSC)

Mutual funds purchased on a deferred sales charge (DSC) do not charge an up-front commission to the client, but the advisor typically receives a 5 percent commission from the fund company. He may also earn an annual trailer fee of about 0.50 percent per year. Once it is purchased, the fund must be held for an average of seven years or a declining redemption penalty will apply. These carry penalties (deferred sales charges) that are usually quite steep if the fund is redeemed in the early years after purchase.

Here is a typical redemption schedule:

Year One = 6%
Year Two = 5.5%
Year Three = 5%
Year Four = 4.5%
Year Five = 3%
Year Six = 1.5%
Year Seven = 0

If an investor intends to hold a mutual fund for the long term (i.e., beyond the expiry of the redemption schedule) then a DSC mutual fund may be the most cost-effective option.

Some considerations before investing in a mutual fund with the deferred sales charge option:

- If you hold a fund for a few years and suddenly the star manager leaves to go to another company, would you or would you not choose to follow him?
- What if you hold a fund that has had poor performance and you want to invest your money elsewhere?

- What if you need access to your money and are faced with an early-redemption penalty?

There is generally no cost for switching funds within the same mutual fund company or if you stay until the redemption schedule expires. However, that may not be your wish.

2. Front-End, or Low-Load

Mutual funds may also be purchased on a front-end or low-load basis. After paying a one-time, up-front commission (typically 0 to 3 percent), the fund can be redeemed, without penalty, at any time.

3. No-Load, or Zero-Load

The third option is to buy a no-load, or zero-load, fund. These funds have no costs associated with the purchase or redemption of units.

Mutual Fund Management Fees (MERs)

The other cost associated with mutual funds is the management expense ratio. This is an annual fee that ranges from less than 1 percent on money market funds to more than 3 percent for some "special" equity funds. Some funds incur management expense ratios as high as 5 percent.

This ongoing charge covers the costs associated with managing the fund, including commissions to trade stocks, research costs, and the fund manager's salary. A proportion of the fee is also paid to the investment advisor for his ongoing contact with the unit holder or client. These costs are listed in your mutual fund prospectus. Make sure to review it carefully.

"Wrap" Accounts

Some wrap accounts, in which brokerage account costs are "wrapped" into a single or fixed fee, can charge you a management fee in addition to the management expense ratios related to the mutual funds they may be investing in. Make sure to inquire about all fees, especially if the programme invests in mutual or other pooled funds, where additional hidden fees may apply.

Performance Fees

Some investment counsellors charge performance fees. Under this arrangement, advisors receive bonuses or are able to charge a higher percentage if the account earns above a certain return. At first glance, this seems to make a lot of sense, as it should motivate the advisor to earn higher returns. However, some advisors may take undue risks with their client's assets in order to seek higher returns and bonuses for themselves.

The type of advisor you chose, the company he works for, and the investment strategy you implement are all factors that will help to determine the payment structure of your account.

It is the advisor's responsibility to disclose all related fees associated with your investments. Make sure to ask questions, and make sure the answers are explained to your satisfaction, so that you fully understand what you are being charged.

— CHAPTER 7 —

How to Evaluate Performance

One of the challenges of investing is that, while an advisor is expected to make money for her clients, she does not have control over, nor can she predict, market performance, especially in the short term. Amateur investors often expect a consistent, positive return. Or, they simply look at the returns of the stock market and expect their performance to be the same or better.

Neither of these presumptions is realistic because of the following:

- It is impossible to predict the outcome of the market.
- Markets are volatile, and returns are not consistent from year to year.

Investing is not an exact science. It is impossible to predict the outcome of the market and to time buys and sells with 100 percent accuracy. Be mindful of anyone who tells you otherwise or who claims to have developed a model to accurately forecast market outcome. Since no one can predict the future, neither can the market be timed.

Accurate market calls (i.e., knowing when to take all your money out of the stock market or when to put it all back in) are based on luck, not skill. Rarely does anyone get this right more than once. Bets on market direction can have huge repercussions, which are often negative, on your overall performance. Remember the caveat that accompanies most published return information: "Past performance does not guarantee future returns." History is useful as a guide to help with long-term trends, but the outcome of two market events in the short term is seldom the same.

Table 1 tracks calendar year returns from 2001–2010.

Market	2010	2009	2008	2007	2006	2005	2004	2003	2002	2001
TSX Composite	14.4	30.7	-35	7.12	14.6	21.91	12.44	24.29	-13.97	-13.87
S&P 500	6.2	7.1	-24.4	-11.34	14	-0.42	1	4.29	-24.39	-7.6
MSCI EAFE (Global)	-1.2	10.8	-32.6	-6.98	23.89	7.18	8.97	11.63	-18.61	-17.76
DEX Bond Universe	6.72	5.41	6.4	3.66	4.08	6.46	7.13	6.69	8.73	8.04

Source: RBC Dominion Securities

Table 1 illustrates why it is unrealistic to aim for a consistent, yearly return. The performance of the indices varied from a low of -35% on the TSX in 2008 to a high of 30.7% on the TSX in 2009.

Let's examine how rates of return are calculated and how to evaluate your overall performance.

Your *absolute* rate of return is the actual rate of return you have earned over a certain time period, usually one year. It is the percentage gain or loss on an investment or account and can be reported before or net of (after) fees. Your absolute rate of return will be a function of your exposure to a number of different criteria, including the following:

- asset mix (i.e., stocks, bonds, and cash)
- security selection
- geographical exposure

What is a realistic expectation of return, and how can you measure and evaluate the performance of your investment advisor and your accounts? This is a very good question. One technique is "*relative* returns." While you may be tempted to judge your performance based on absolute figures (e.g., wanting a 10 percent return), you should evaluate your returns on relative performance.

Relative performance measures your returns compared to the indices of the markets you are investing in, or benchmarks. This method is referred to as "benchmarking" and is the industry standard for institutional investors like pension funds. For example, the returns of a portfolio invested in US stocks should be measured against the S&P 500. If the index earned -25%, then a return in that vicinity is realistic, although disappointing in absolute terms. If the benchmark or index has declined 10 percent and your account is down 8 percent, then on a relative basis, your portfolio has done well—this despite the fact that you have suffered a loss.

Furthermore, if you have 50 percent exposure to the S&P 500 and 50 percent in treasury bills, then your portfolio should be measured against a benchmark that is 50 percent S&P 500 and 50 percent treasury bill index. This is called a benchmark portfolio. A benchmark portfolio is a portfolio with the same asset mix as yours, using the appropriate indices. The returns of a portfolio that is divided into, say, 10% cash, 40% Canadian stocks, and 50% fixed income should therefore be measured against a benchmark portfolio of 10% treasury bill index, 40% TSX 60, and 50% DS Barra Bond Index.

However, benchmarking has its limitations. It is unlikely for an investor to own all listed companies and in the same proportion as the index. In aiming for the benchmark return, investors must assume the same amount of risk as the market, which may be significantly higher than their comfort level reasonably allows.

No advisor will outperform in every period or even every year. If you have not done as well as the benchmark, it is unreasonable to expect to earn the same return as the market if you are not prepared to assume the same amount of risk. For example, in order to have matched the returns of the TSX in the late 1990s you would have had to hold more than 30 percent of your portfolio in Northern Telecom, which collapsed a few years later. In 2007, the TSX earned 7.12%, but the ten best performing stocks in the TSX accounted for all of the gain. This means the remaining fifty stocks in the index generated a negative return for the year.[12] Most advisors would not recommend having substantial overweight position in any company, which might lead to periodic underperformance when the market weighting is skewed to favour only a few stocks.

One of the most valuable skills of an advisor lies not only in his ability to make money in good markets ("Do not confuse luck for brains," as the saying goes!). Rather, it is the ability to outperform in a bad market. To grow your capital over time, it is essential to minimize your losses. If you suffer a 50 percent loss in your account, you now need to earn 100 percent, or double your money, to recover. The right advisor should earn you a reasonably consistent return over an extended period of time. Avoid the temptation to judge advisors solely on rates of return. Similarly, do not necessarily believe people who like to talk about how much money they have made in the market. Some people love to talk about gains, but they never mention their losses.

You should also consider that everyone has different objectives and tolerances for risk. Generally speaking, higher-risk investments may offer a potential for higher returns, but the chances of greater losses are also true. A lower rate of return may be suitable for more

---

12   RBC Dominion Securities, "Year in Review," printed Wed., January 16, 2008.

conservative investors, given their objectives and lower tolerance for risk.

Therefore, the benchmarking method should be used only as a guide.

I often ask new clients what rate of return they would like to earn. The most common answer I hear is 10 percent. In the 1980s and early 1990s, this was achievable because interest rates and inflation were abnormally high. When those decades are factored out of long-term historical returns, you see that there was hardly any other period in the twentieth century when returns were that high.

In order to determine a reasonable expectation of return, we need to examine the rates of return of various markets over a long-term period that is still recent enough to be relevant today. Let's look at some actual returns over a number of different time periods. I have chosen the median Canadian balanced mutual fund (i.e., the fund right in the middle—50 percent of funds are above and 50 percent are below) to represent the typical portfolio of a moderate investor.

Table 2 tracks the performance of different markets over a twenty-year period.

Table 2 Market Return over a Twenty-Year Period

Fund	5-Year Return (%)	10-Year Return (%)	15-Year Return (%)	20-Year Return (%)
Median Canadian Balanced Fund*	3.7	3.7	6.2	–
Market				
DEX 91-Day T-Bill Return Canada	2.54	2.8	3.39	4.29
S&P TSX Composite Total Return	7.0	5.1	9.44	9.8
S&P 500 Total Return	1.7	-0.02	6.74	9.28
DEX Bond Universe Index	5.81	6.74	7.2	8.64
MSCI EAFE Index (Global)	0.57	0.75	2.82	3.4

Source: RBC Dominion Securities

*Morningstar Research

Over a ten-year period (from 2000 to 2010), the TSX earned a total annual return of 5.1 percent, and the S&P 500 lost .02 percent. The DEX bond index earned 6.74 percent. Even over the twenty-year period, not one of the listed markets earned 10 percent. Therefore, in a similar economic environment, such an expectation of return would be a highly unrealistic goal.

As a rule of thumb, many financial planners use the historical, long-term rate of return of about 6.5 percent in their projections for a balanced portfolio.

Establishing an acceptable rate of return will be a function of your personal objectives, time horizon, and tolerance for risk. Therefore, you will need to discuss performance with your advisor on an individual basis.

While performance is important, it is only one of the criteria that should be used in evaluating an investment advisor. Non-market related issues that he can control need to be examined, such as the level of service and support. Some of these factors were addressed in chapter 5.

— CHAPTER 8 —
Making It Work: Forming Realistic Expectations

Ultimately, a successful relationship with your advisor is based on having realistic expectations concerning what he is capable of providing for you and recognizing his limitations.

Here are some important factors to help you create realistic expectations of what your advisor can and cannot do:

1. Do not blame your advisor for bad markets.

Some investors change advisors every few years or whenever there is a market correction. This is because they blame their advisors—not the market—for their poor performance, as if their advisors should somehow have been able to predict the events before they happened.

2. Understand how to measure and evaluate rate of return.

During the credit crisis of 2008–2009, many investors were disappointed with their returns. This is completely understandable, as the market experienced two years of unprecedented volatility, in addition to one of the biggest declines in fifty years. Instead of accepting perfectly acceptable relative returns, which were low as a result of market conditions, however, many deviated from their long-term investment discipline or strategy. One of the only ways to attempt to earn higher returns, if the market did not improve, was to increase the exposure to risk in their portfolio. This could potentially lead to better performance, but it could also lead to a substantial loss of capital. Therefore, returns need to be assessed on a risk-adjusted basis.

3. Do not expect your advisor to be able to predict market outcome.[13]

Hindsight is always twenty-twenty, and it is easy to say, "We all saw the market decline coming." Even if the advisor did, you must remember that no one rings a bell at the top and at the bottom of the market. The biggest risk to market timing is not about knowing when to get out but, rather, when to get back in. Therefore, you have to make not one but two right calls. While many panicked investors liquidated their holdings during the credit crisis of 2008 and 2009, few were able to successfully reinvest at the bottom. As a result, they sat in cash while the market recovered—substantially!

---

13 http://www.osc.gov.on.ca/documents/en/Investors/res_working-with -adviser_en.pdf, accessed July 8, 2011.

4. Do not expect your advisor to make you rich.

I often tell my clients that it is their job to make the money. It is my job to manage it.

5. Do not expect your advisor to recommend investments that are always profitable.[14] It is reasonable to expect your advisor to be right more often than he is wrong. Over time, you should average an acceptable rate of return.

6. Do not expect your advisor to buy a stock at its lowest price or sell it at its all-time high.

7. Do not expect that your advisor will have access to inside knowledge.

Advisors do not have such knowledge. Even if they did, they are prohibited from disseminating or acting on it. It is illegal—end of story.

8. Accept that your advisor will not be able to meet unrealistic goals or expectations of profit.[15]

9. Do not expect your advisor to work for free. There are circumstances in which discounts are appropriate. But remember the old adage: "you get what you pay for."

---

14   http://www.osc.gov.on.ca/documents/en/Investors/res_working-with
      -adviser_en.pdf, accessed July 8, 2011.
15   http://www.osc.gov.on.ca/documents/en/Investors/res_working-with
      -adviser_en.pdf, accessed July 8, 2011.

10. Do not always correlate fees with performance.

You are not paying your advisor to make you money all the time. Advisors work just as hard, if not harder, in a difficult or declining market. Do you pay your accountant according to the size of your tax bill?

— CHAPTER 9 —

Keys to a Successful Relationship

Although you may have hired an advisor because you do not have the time to manage your investments or because you are not interested in the stock market, at the end of the day, it is your money. In order to accomplish your financial goals, you, the investor, have some responsibilities.

- Recognize that the relationship with your advisor is a partnership, a two-way street. The more your advisor knows about you and your circumstances, goals, and risk tolerance, the better he can serve you. You must be open and upfront with your advisor in terms of your full financial picture. While this information may seem overly personal, it is critical for determining an investment plan that is suited to meet all of your needs.

- Advisors appreciate clients who are clear and honest about their financial situation and expectations, because it means they can give better advice. Remember, you are paying for this advice. Ultimately, you have to make the decisions and live with the results.[16]

- If anything material in your life changes and will affect your financial plan, be sure to let your advisor know as soon as possible.
- Review statements, return your advisor's calls, and make time to meet with him.
- Your advisor is not a mind reader. If you have any questions or concerns, call him.
- Take advantage of the services offered by your advisor and his firm. Investment, tax, and estate planning are essential components of your overall financial well-being.
- Trust your advisor and do not be swayed by the media or common sentiment.

---

16   Canadian Securities Administrators. "Working with a Financial Advisor." http://www.securities.adminstrators.ca/uploadedfiles/general /pdfs/choosing_advisors_brochure.pdf.

— CHAPTER 10 —

The Financial Services Industry in Canada

Until recently, the financial services industry in Canada was divided into four distinct areas, each with its own defined regulations. They were known as the "four pillars of financial services" and were broken down into the following industry groups:

1. Banks
2. Trust Companies
3. Brokerage Firms
4. Insurance Companies

In 1987, sweeping changes to the rules resulted in a complete overhaul of the system. The new legislation allowed banks to merge with trust companies and to buy brokerage firms. It also permitted insurance companies to accept deposits (like bank savings accounts) and for banks to create insurance divisions. Today, financial firms are able to provide products and services that were once well beyond the scope of their original responsibilities. No wonder it is so confusing.

Using the chart below, I will help you to understand today's structure of financial services companies as well as the products and services they can provide.

Institution	Products	Services
I. Banks *		
1) Bank Branch	GICs (Guaranteed Investment Certificates) mutual funds (usually proprietary; i.e., their own bank funds)	Basic financial and retirement planning
2) Full-Service Broker	Third party mutual funds, broad range of GICs, stocks bonds, new issues, Initial Public Offerings (IPOs), Exchange Traded Funds (ETFs), derivatives, insurance products	Investment management on a discretionary and non- discretionary basis, comprehensive financial planning, tax support, insurance, will and estate consulting, access to research
3) Discount Broker	Third party mutual funds, broad range of GICs, stocks, bonds, ETFs	Self-directed trade execution with access to research
4) Private Trust or Counsel	Pooled funds, segregated stock and bond portfolios	Discretionary investment management only, comprehensive financial planning, tax support, insurance, will and estate consulting
II. Independent Brokerage Firms	Third party mutual funds, broad range of GICs, stocks, bonds, new issues, IPOs, ETFs, derivatives, insurance products	Comprehensive financial planning, tax support, will and estate consulting, insurance, access to research

III. Independent Investment Counsellor	Pooled funds, segregated stock and bond portfolios	Discretionary investment management only, comprehensive financial planning, tax planning, will and estate consulting
IV. Financial/ Retirement Planning Firms and Mutual Fund Companies	Mutual funds, GICs; some have limited access to stocks and bonds	Basic financial and retirement planning

*Some banks also have insurance divisions

As you can see from the above chart, you have many options to choose from, both in terms of the kind of company to deal with, as well as products and services available to you.

Through their branch banking system and through ownership of brokerage and private counsel firms and trusts, Canadian banks are the largest investment managers in Canada. With billions of dollars under management and thousands of clients served, Canadian banks are able to offer the most comprehensive investment resources to investors.

The right choice will depend on the complexity of your needs at different stages in your life. Depending on your circumstances, you may choose to deal with one or more financial services companies throughout your lifetime.

— CHAPTER 11 —
Advisor Credentials and Designations

The descriptions and functions of the various investment advisors do have specific meanings, but there is considerable misunderstanding about them and some are used interchangeably. For example, "financial advisor" is a general term that can describe a broad range of service providers, the financial planning function can be used in association with other services, and licensed investment advisors and investment counsellors do similar work

In this chapter, I will discuss the regulatory organizations which license the various sectors of the industry, and then on the chart on page 64, I will describe the three main types of advisors, along with their titles and functions.

Advisors can work at places like banks, financial planning firms, brokerage firms, and investment management firms. Not all advisors offer the same products and services, nor do they have the same expertise. Some specialize in certain kinds of investments; others can offer you a wide range of investments and services.[17]

It is crucial to be able to understand and distinguish between all of the initials following an advisor's name on his business card.

It is a good idea to choose a firm that is a member of one of Canada's self-regulatory organizations (SROs)—such as the Investment Industry Regulators Organization of Canada (IIROC) or the Mutual Fund Dealers Association (MFDA)—and whose employees are registered. Registration helps protect investors, because securities regulators will only register firms and individuals if they are properly qualified. Firms and individuals are registered by category, and each category has different education and experience requirements and permits different activities.[18]

An advisor's registration is more important than his title, because it tells you the type of products or services he is able to offer. As discussed above, people registered as mutual fund dealers can sell and provide product advice on mutual funds, but they are not qualified to handle other investments. To a certain degree, the firm the investment advisor is employed by will provide clues to the advisor's qualifications and vice versa. An investment counsellor is unlikely to work for a financial planning company that sells mutual funds, because he would be overqualified to do so. Conversely, the mutual fund salesperson is not qualified to manage money on a discretionary basis. An employee of a

---

17   Canadian Securities Administrators. "Working with a Financial Advisor." http://www.osc.gov.on.ca/documents/en/Investors/res_working-with-adviser_en.pdf, accessed July 8, 2011.

18   Canadian Securities Institute Global Education. "Choosing the Right Investment Advisor: Things You Should Know." https://www.csi.ca/student/en_ca/home.xhtml, accessed July 8, 2011.

full-service brokerage firm is required to complete a minimum number of courses and is encouraged to complete several others. A chartered life underwriter (i.e., an insurance agent) is unlikely to have had his Canadian Securities Course (although he may), nor is he likely to have completed the CPH (Conduct and Practices Handbook Examination).

Some of the major designations and licenses currently available by regulator are as follows:

1. Investment Industry Regulatory Organization of Canada-IIROC (formerly IDA) members. These government agencies regulate investment dealers and brokerage firms with the following designations:
   a. Canadian investment manager (CIM)
   b. registered representative, options
   c. registered representative, futures contracts
   d. portfolio manager
2. Securities commissions members: investment counsellor/portfolio manager (ICPM)
3. Association for Investment Management and Research (AIMR): chartered financial analyst (CFA)
4. Institute of Canadian Bankers (ICB): personal financial planner (PFP)
5. Mutual Fund Dealers Association of Canada: MFDA license
6. Financial Planning Standards Council (FPSC): certified financial planner (CFP)
7. Financial Advisors Association of Canada: chartered life underwriter (CLU)

As the investment industry continues to evolve, so do licensing requirements. For this reason, I encourage you to check with your local regulator to ensure that the information you have is accurate and up-to-date.

The chart below lists the major investment advisory services providers as well as the positions of their employees and some of the designations those employees may hold. Definitions of the designations are provided in the glossary at the back of the book.

Institution	Employee Title or Position	Advisor Designations
I. Banks		
1) Bank Branch	account manager investments, financial planner, IRP	Certified Financial Planner (CFP), mutual fund license, PFP
2) Full-Service Broker (Bank Owned)	investment, financial, or wealth advisor, investment executive	CSC/CPH, CIM/PMT, CFP, Options, Futures
3) Full-Service Broker (Independent)	portfolio manager, discretionary money manager	discretionary license(CIM,PMT,CFA), Options, Futures
4) Private Trust or Counsel	portfolio manager/ investment counsellor	discretionary license (CIM,PMT,CFA), Options, Futures
II. Investment Counsellor	portfolio manager/ investment counsellor	discretionary license (CIM,PMT,CFA), Options, Futures
III. Financial/ Retirement Planning Firms	financial planners	CFP, mutual fund license

The chart on page 64 can be summarized into three main types of advisors:

1. financial planners or mutual fund salespeople
2. licensed investment advisors (traditionally referred to as stockbrokers)
3. investment counsellors or portfolio managers

1. Financial Planners

The terms *financial planner* and *financial advisor* are often used interchangeably. Yet, it is important to note that they are not one and the same. While many in the industry refer to themselves as financial planners, technically only those with the CFP designation are permitted to do so. *Financial advisor*, on the other hand, is not a designation and can be used to describe a broad range of financial services providers.

For a fee, an independent financial planner will help you with issues like budgeting and will design a plan for you. He does not implement the investment strategy. Rather, he would then refer you to someone with the appropriate investment management experience, like a licensed investment advisor or portfolio manager.

Many planners work for companies that sell mutual funds. They prepare financial plans at little or no cost. They are compensated by implementing the investment component through the sale of mutual funds. Many mutual fund salespeople fall under this category.

Unlike investment advisors licensed with the Exchange, the majority of financial planners are licensed to sell mutual funds only.

2. Licensed Investment Advisors

The Investment Industry Regulators Organization of Canada (IIROC) regulates companies in the brokerage industry and monitors their employees' licenses. This is accomplished by ensuring they are proficient with the required industry courses for each applicable license to deal with the investing public. There are a multitude of accreditations and certifications. Many requirements are mandated by the employer, who, in turn, is regulated by a specific agency.

The rules for becoming a licensed investment advisor in Canada are some of the most stringent in the world. An investment advisor must be registered with the provincial securities commission to sell securities. Before he can be registered, he must pass the Canadian Securities Course and the Conduct and Practices Handbook Exam, both offered by the Canadian Securities Institute. New investment advisors must also complete ninety-day training programmes provided by their employers. After that, the investment advisors are supervised closely and have to complete an additional investment course (Wealth Management Essentials). They are also required to complete continuing education courses throughout their career.[19] Regulators provide guidelines, and most firms have their own internal policies. Some of these courses may include topics like the following:

---

19   Canadian Securities Institute Global Education. "Choosing the Right Investment Advisor: Things You Should Know." https://www.csi.ca /student/en_ca/home.xhtml, accessed July 8, 2011.

- investment management,
- product knowledge,
- ethics,
- money laundering,
- compliance, and
- insurance training (if licensed).

3. Investment Counsellor or Portfolio Managers

These advisors both manage money on a discretionary basis. A portfolio manager is licensed by the IIROC and usually works for a brokerage firm. An investment counsellor is licensed by his provincial securities commission and is typically employed by a private trust or investment counselling firm.

The portfolio or discretionary money manager (PM) is the gold standard of investment advisors. In this arrangement, the portfolio manager makes the day-to-day decisions in accounts, based on guidelines discussed with the client and on a written agreement called an investment policy statement (IPS). Since the client relies on the PM to make all investment-related decisions on his or her behalf, the PM is held to the highest standard of care. He is fully accountable to the client. Because of the additional responsibility entrusted to the portfolio manager, only a select group of advisors qualifies for the designation. To become a portfolio manager, a candidate applying for the designation is typically evaluated and appointed based on a number of criteria, including the following:

- advanced investment credentials

- years of experience advising clients
- dollar value of assets under administration
- investment discipline
- clean compliance record

Portfolio managers, like those employed by full-service brokerage firms, are qualified to provide a broad range of investment-related products and services. For this reason, they are often the best choice for sophisticated or high-net-worth investors.

In summary, the licensing and designation of the individual you are considering are two essential components in qualifying his calibre of expertise. Make sure you have an understanding of each designation and what it means; this will help you to evaluate the credentials of advisors you are considering.

CONCLUSION

As I have pointed out, there are many considerations in developing your overall investment strategy. The first step is to investigate and to learn—to know yourself and how you can best deal with the intricacies of the financial markets; to decide what you need; and to learn about the different types of advisors and their qualifications.

In all aspects of our lives, whether it relates to helping our families, working on our finances, or dealing with health issues, we value the expertise of skilled professionals. If you had a broken leg, would you want to be treated by a general practitioner or an orthopaedic surgeon?

Whether you are at the early stages of accumulating wealth, in the consolidation phase of your investments, or in retirement and looking to reap the fruits of a successful financial plan, the right advisor will guide you to reach your long-term goals.

Hopefully this book has been able to sort through the complex information relating to the investment services industry and explain it in a way that makes sense to you.

You *deserve* the best and are entitled to a successful long-term partnership with your advisor. After making the right choice, you will have peace of mind and will feel confident about your financial future.

Glossary

This glossary is reprinted with permission from the Canadian Securities Administrators.[20]

balanced portfolio.	an investment portfolio that holds an appropriate mix of different types of investments, such as bonds and shares
bond.	an investment in which a government or company promises to repay money borrowed from investors at a specified time and to pay interest at a specified rate
budget.	an estimate of the income and expenses of a person, a family, or an organization over a certain period of time
Canada Deposit Insurance Corporation.	a federal governmental organization that provides insurance to protect money deposited in Canadian banks and certain other financial institutions
Canadian investment manager.	designation (CIM) from the Canadian Securities Institute that requires that candidates complete courses in Canadian Securities and investment and portfolio management. Advisors with this designation can sell mutual funds.

20   Canadian Securities Administrators. "Working with a Financial Advisor." http://www.osc.gov.on.ca/documents/en/Investors/res_working-with -adviser_en.pdf, accessed July 7, 2011.

Canadian Investor Protection Fund.	a Canadian not-for-profit organization set up by the investment industry that is designed to protect investors from the bankruptcy of an individual investment firm. Accounts are covered for up to $1 million in shortfall of securities, commodity and futures contracts, segregated insurance funds, and cash.
Canadian Securities Administrators.	a council of the securities regulators from Canada's thirteen provinces and territories
cash account.	a trading account from which you pay cash for all transactions
cash equivalent.	an investment, such as a treasury bill, that can be converted quickly to cash with little risk
certified financial planner.	the internationally recognized designation (CFP) awarded in Canada by Financial Planners Standards Council. Certified financial planners must meet the Financial Planners Standards Council's standards in education, experience, examination, and ethics. Certified financial planners must also have thirty hours of continuing education every year and agree to abide by the certified financial planner code of ethics to renew their right to use the designation annually.
chartered financial analyst.	designation (CFA) issued by the Association for Investment Management and Research. Candidates must pass three levels of exams in areas including accounting, economics, ethics, money management, and security analysis. Candidates must have three years of experience and a bachelor's degree.
commission.	a fee you pay to a broker or agent for the service of arranging the purchase or sale of a security or real estate investment. The amount of commission varies between brokers.
common share.	a share in the ownership of a company that gives the holder a vote in the election of directors and some other major corporate decisions (see equities, shares, stocks)

compound interest.	interest that is paid based on the original amount deposited as well as on any interest that has been earned in previous periods (e.g., in year one, the bank pays you five dollars in interest on your one hundred-dollar deposit; in year two, it pays you interest on $105)
dealers.	people who are registered to buy or sell securities on behalf of clients and who give advice to clients about the purchase or sale of securities. Some dealers are registered with a self-regulatory organization like the Investment Industry Regulatory Organization of Canada and the Mutual Fund Dealers Association of Canada.
debenture.	similar to a bond; a loan for a specific term during which repayment is secured by the general credit of the borrower
deposit insurance.	an insurance plan designed to protect the money you deposit if a bank, credit union, or trust company fails (see Canada Deposit Insurance Corporation)
discount brokerage firm.	brokerage firms that charge a lower fee, compared to fees of a full-service broker, to buy and sell securities but provide no investment advice
discretionary trade.	when you give someone else (usually your portfolio manager) the authority to make investment decisions and trade securities for you without checking with you on each trade
dividend.	a portion of a company's profits that is paid to shareholders
equities.	shares in a company
expected return.	the overall profit you expect to receive from an investment in the future; may be very different from the actual returns that you eventually receive
financial advisor.	a person who offers advice about buying or selling investments
financial institution.	a bank, trust company, credit union, or other institution that offers financial services, such as savings and chequing accounts, loans, and credit cards

financial plan.	a written plan that helps you identify your goals and figure out how to manage your money to achieve them
financial planners.	people who determine how individuals can meet their goals through proper management of their financial resources. Financial planners offer financial services such as budgeting, cash and debt management, and retirement and tax planning. They cannot trade securities or recommend investments to their clients, unless they are registered with the provincial securities regulator in their province. Some financial planners are registered to trade in mutual funds and segregated funds (an insurance product).
fixed income investments.	investments, such as government and corporate bonds, debentures and preferred shares, that give you fixed interest or dividend income
guaranteed investment certificate.	an investment in which you deposit money with a financial institution for a fixed period of time and receive a specified rate of interest.
investment account statement.	a record of transactions and balances in an account at an investment firm; usually issued monthly
Investment Dealers Association of Canada.	consolidated in 2008 with Market Regulation Services, Inc., to form the Investment Industry Regulatory Organization of Canada (see IIRPC)
investment firm.	a company that buys and sells investments for its clients
Investment Industry Regulatory Organization of Canada.	the national self-regulatory organization that oversees all investment dealers and trading activity on debt and equity marketplaces in Canada. Created in 2008 through the consolidation of the Investment Dealers Association of Canada and Market Regulation Services, Inc., the Investment Industry Regulators Organization of Canada sets high-quality regulatory and investment industry standards, protects investors, and strengthens market integrity while maintaining efficient and competitive capital markets.

issuer.	a company or other entity that has issued or is proposing to issue securities
know your client rule.	requirement that ensures that advisors know detailed information about their clients' individual risk tolerance, investment knowledge, and financial position. This information is collected on forms designed to protect both clients and advisors.
liquidity	ability to sell an investment quickly and at a fair price
margin account.	a trading account that allows you to borrow money on securities you currently own or intend to purchase
Market Regulation Services, Inc.	consolidated in 2008 with the Investment Dealers Association of Canada to form the Investment Industry Regulatory Organization of Canada (see IIROC)
maturity date.	the date on which a bond, debenture, guaranteed investment certificate or term deposit is due to be repaid
mutual fund.	a pool of money that is invested for a large number of investors by a professional money manager
mutual fund dealer.	a company that buys and sells the shares or units of mutual funds for investors
Mutual Fund Dealers Association of Canada.	the national self-regulatory organization for the distribution side of the Canadian mutual fund industry. The mutual fund dealers association of Canada regulates the operations, standards of practice, and business conduct of its members and their representatives.
mutual fund unit.	part ownership in a mutual fund
National Registration Database.	the Canadian Securities Administrators' national web-based system that permits individuals who are dealers or advisors to file registration forms electronically. Investors can check whether an individual or firm is registered to sell investments.
order.	a decision issued by a securities regulatory authority under the securities regulation of the relevant province or territory

pension.	a regular payment, usually from a fund that the employer and employee have contributed to in prior years, made to a retired or disabled employee
personal financial planner.	the banking industry's equivalent of certified financial planner. To earn this designation (PFP), which is administered by the Institute of Canadian Bankers, bank/financial institution employees must complete a financial planning educational program and have a minimum of six months of work experience.
portfolio.	the bundle of stocks, bonds, or other investments you hold
portfolio manager.	person who is authorized to make discretionary trades for you. Sometimes investors allow their portfolio managers to make discretionary trades on their behalf.
principal.	the money originally invested or lent to earn interest or other income
prospectus.	a formal document required by law when a company wants to sell shares to the public
provincial securities commissions.	the regulatory agency responsible for administering a province's securities laws
real return.	the return from an investment after taking inflation into account (e.g., if your investment earned 6 percent interest the year before, but the cost of living increased by 4 percent, you would only be ahead by 2 percent; your real return is only 2 percent)
registered.	advisors and investment companies licensed by a securities regulator to buy and sell investments or advise on investments; also accounts and retirement plans protected by income tax and other laws
registered education savings plan.	a special type of savings plan registered with the government that allows you to reduce the taxes you pay on money you save for postsecondary education expenses.

registered financial planner.	a designation (RFP) administered by the Financial Advisors Association of Canada—Advocis (formerly the Canadian Association of Financial Planners), a non-regulatory, voluntary membership body; no educational program is necessary, but passing an exam is required
registered retirement income fund.	a tax deferral investment available to holders of a registered retirement savings plan who unregister their plans. The plan holder invests withdrawn registered retirement savings plan funds in the registered retirement income fund and must withdraw and pay income tax on a set portion of the fund each year.
registered retirement savings plan.	a special type of savings plan registered with the government that allows you to reduce the income tax you pay on money you save for retirement. Any income you earn in the registered retirement savings plan is usually exempt from tax for the time the funds remain in the plan. During retirement, a registered retirement savings plan can be another source of income.
risk tolerance.	how willing to or comfortable with risking losing your money on an investment and the extent to which you are comfortable with volatility
savings account.	an account with a bank, trust company, or credit union that pays interest on the money you deposit and allows you to withdraw your money at any time
securities.	transferable certificates of ownership of investment products including bonds, notes, stocks, future contracts, and options
self-regulatory organizations.	organizations like the Investment Industry Regulatory Organization of Canada and the Mutual Fund Dealers Association of Canada, which make sure their member firms meet standards set by provincial laws for securities
share.	stock; a certificate that represents part ownership of a company
shareholder.	someone who owns shares in a company

shortfall.	the difference between the market value of an account and what an insolvent company can return to the customer
stock.	a share in the ownership of a company
stock exchange.	a place where shares and some other types of investments can be bought and sold
trade.	a trade is the disposition of a security for valuable consideration. It does not include the purchase of a security or a transfer, pledge, or mortgage or other encumbrance of a security for the purpose of giving collateral for debt.
term deposit.	a type of deposit with a financial institution that is repaid to you at a specified time (e.g., ninety days or one year) and at a specified interest rate
trust company.	a financial institution, similar to a bank, that can take deposits and make loans; trust companies often provide other specialized services, like administering estates and pension plans, that banks cannot
Toronto Stock Exchange.	a subsidiary of TSX Group

Useful Contact Information

Canadian Securities Administrators
www.securities-administrators.ca

Investment Industry Regulators Organization of Canada
www.iiroc.ca

Here is a list of websites and phone numbers for the provincial members of the Canadian Securities Administrators:

Ontario Securities Commission
www.osc.gov.on.ca
(416) 593-8314
(877) 785-1555

Prince Edward Island Office of the Attorney General
www.gov.pe.ca/securities
(902) 368-4550

Autorité des marches financiers (Québec)
www.lautorite.qc.ca
(877) 525-0337
(514) 395-0337

Financial Services Regulation Division, Newfoundland and Labrador
www.gs.gov.nl.ca
(709) 729-4189

Nova Scotia Securities Commission
www.gov.ns.ca/nssc
(902) 424-7768

New Brunswick Securities Commission
www.nbsc-cvmnb.ca
(506) 658-3060
(866) 933-2222 (NB only)

Manitoba Securities Commission
www.msc.gov.mb.ca
(204) 945-2548
(800) 655-5244 (MB only)

Saskatchewan Financial Services Commission
www.sfsc.gov.sk.ca
(306) 787-5645

Alberta Securities Commission
www.albertasecurities.com
(403) 297-6454
(877) 355-4488

British Columbia Securities Commission
www.investright.org
(604) 899-6854
(800) 373-6393 (BC and AB only)

Northwest Territories Registrar of Securities
www.justice.gov.nt.ca/SecuritiesRegistry
(867) 920-3318

Nunavut Registrar of Securities
www.gov.nu.ca
(867) 975-6587

Yukon Registrar of Securities
www.gov.yk.ca/corp/secureinvest.html
(867) 667-5225

NOTES

NOTES

NOTES

NOTES

NOTES

NOTES

NOTES